DRAWING DATA WITH KIDS

Gulrez Khan

DRAWING DATA WITH KIDS
Copyright © 2023 Gulrez Khan
All rights reserved.

ISBN: 9798391557739

All rights reserved.
No part of this publication may be reproduced,
stored in a retrieval system, distributed or
transmitted in any form or by any means without
prior written permission from the publisher.

DEDICATION

To my better half, Farhat who continues to amaze and inspire me each and every day.

A NOTE BEFORE WE BEGIN

As a parent, I know how important it is to prepare our children for the future. And in today's digital age, it means equipping them with the skills they need to succeed in a data-driven world. However, my beloved wife often reminds me of the importance of ensuring our children have a childhood full of screen-free, family bonding experiences.

That's why I wrote 'Drawing Data with Kids'. This book not only teaches about data and ways to visualize it, but it also weaves in stories and gives ideas for how families can create interest in data and promote screen-free bonding experiences.

I believe learning should be engaging and enjoyable, which is why I've filled this book with stories that will keep children interested while teaching them valuable skills.

You'll follow Pariza and her family on their adventures as they explore the world of Data Visualization. Pariza is a bright and energetic 10-year-old girl with a passion for learning and creativity. She loves to dress up like her mom and play pretend teacher to her younger brother. Her father, who she calls "Abbu," is a data-nerd, always looking for excuses to introduce his kids to data visualization. He works from home and is often around to answer Pariza's many questions.

Along the way, you'll learn how to turn everyday data into beautiful visualizations that tell a story. You'll also discover how easy it can be to incorporate data literacy into your family's everyday life.

So, whether you're a parent looking to give your child a head start in the world of data, a schoolteacher looking for interesting ways to keep your students engaged or simply someone interested in the art of data visualization, I invite you to join me and Pariza on this journey. Together, we'll explore the world of data, one graph at a time.

HOW THIS BOOK IS ORGANIZED

In this book, each chapter has a <u>Story</u>, a <u>Time Out</u> section and <u>Your Turn to Play</u>.

Story with real-life example of leveraging Data Visualization:

Stories are immensely powerful! They have the ability to capture the attention of both children and adults alike. That's why in every chapter I have added a story where a Data Visualization is shown that can be used in a real-life situation.

To keep it relatable, each chapter kicks off with the story of Pariza and her Abbu. Abbu's always looking for ways to introduce Pariza to new data visualization concepts, cleverly weaving them into everyday scenarios.

By seeing these techniques in action, I hope readers will gain a deeper understanding of the power and potential of data visualization.

Time Out:

Throughout the book, you'll come across a special section called "Time Out." These segments provide extra details and insights about the graphs introduced in each chapter. So, keep an eye out for them, as they'll help deepen your understanding and appreciation of the power of data visualization.

Your Turn to Play:

Each chapter concludes with an interactive section called "Your Turn to Play." Here, readers will find exercises and activities designed to put their newfound knowledge into practice. These engaging exercises will help reinforce the concepts covered in each chapter.

My hope is that by organizing the book in this manner, readers will have a fun and engaging learning experience.

CONTENTS

01 THE SNORE GRAPH 1
      Waking up early
      Line Graph

02 MONDAY BLUES 7
      Monday Monster
      What is Data
      Day of the Week
      Bar Graph
      Misspelling Wednesdays

03 MONDAY BLUES II 17
      Line Graph with sequence
      Monday is just like Sunday

04 INK-SPARING INSIGHTS 27
      Jogging in the Park
      Running out of Ink
      Months of the Year
      Horizontal Bar Graph

05 SNAKES & LADDERS 37
      Broken LEGO buildings
      More snakes than ladders?
      Pie Chart
      Watermelon Pizza

06 SNAKES & LADDERS II 45
      Walking quietly
      Scatter Plot
      Snakes & Ladders Quadrants

07 PARATHA PATTERNS 55
    Different shapes of Parathas
    Square, Rectangle & Parallelogram
    Scatter Plot

08 BOARD GAME NIGHT 65
    Losing to Priya
    Analyzing the game
    Bar Graph to compare the scores

09 BOARD GAME NIGHT II 75
    Mango Man
    Running Total
    Line Graph
    Triple-Point tile

10 SCRABBLE INSIGHTS 85
    Rainy Day
    Scrabble with the Family
    Line Graph
    Analyzing scores

11 HEATMAP ON A RAINY DAY 95
    Pitter-Patter of rain drops
    Map of USA
    Number if letters in each state
    Creating a heatmap

12 MAPS & CHERRY BLOSSOMS 105
    Martial Arts in the backyard
    Remembering Seattle
    Cherry Blossoms in US
    Physical data visualization

01 THE SNORE GRAPH

Pariza was fast asleep in her bed when she heard a loud thud on her roof. She jumped out of the bed and looked around. 'What was that?' She muttered to herself and looked out the window, but it was too dark.

'I think a branch fell from the tree,' Pariza said to herself.

She tried going back to sleep but couldn't stop thinking about different sounds she was hearing.

Ticking of the clock on her nightstand

'Tick-tock, tick-tock, tick-tock, tick-tock...'

Distant chirping of the crickets.

'Chirp-chirp, chirp-chirp, chirp-chirp, chirp-chirp'.

However, there was one sound that she found funny and fascinating at the same time. It was the snoring of her Abbu (father) coming from the other room.

He snored like a bear, loud and rhythmic. She could imagine his chest rising and falling with each breath.

With everyone asleep and not knowing what else to do, Pariza started doodling the Snore Graph of Abbu.

The Snore Graph

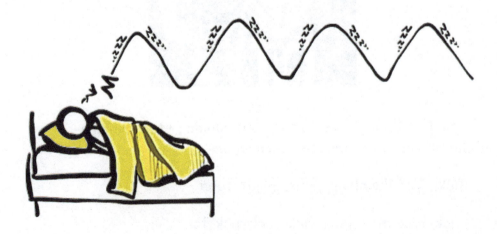

Time Out!

The graph used to describe Abbu's snoring is called a Line Graph.

A Line Graph is a graphical representation of information that changes over a period of time or a sequence.

You can see that the snoring of Abbu starts off quietly, then gets louder and louder, before fading off again and the pattern keeps repeating.

You will see more examples of Line Graphs in further chapters - Chapter 3 (Monday Blues II), Chapter 9 (Board Game Night II) and Chapter 10 (Scrabble Insights).

Pariza was so focused on her drawing that she didn't notice Abbu standing at the door. He was looking at her with a soft smile on his face.

"Why are you up so late, Pariza? Looks like you are drawing something interesting?"

Pariza looked up at him and grinned.

"I'm drawing a graph, just like you do, Abbu!" she said proudly, showing him her drawing.

Looking at the Snore Graph, Abbu couldn't help laughing.

"This is hilarious, Pariza!" he exclaimed, unable to control his laughter.

"You definitely have a future in data visualization!"

Your turn to Play

It was a chilly day, and a gush of wind came from the open window. Abbu sneezed loudly, causing Pariza to jump. 'Achoo! Achoo!'

He sneezed once, then twice, then thrice in quick succession. Pariza saw a pattern in his sneezing. It seemed similar to what she had observed in his snoring. It had a sudden increase in volume followed by a rapid decline.

Can you help Pariza draw a line graph of Abbu's 'Sneeze fit'?

- The Sneeze Graph

- Here are some other examples you can try:
    - Crying Baby Graph
    - Laughing Monster Graph
    - Meow-Meow Graph
    - The Roar Graph

- Do you see any patterns in these graphs?

02 MONDAY BLUES

Pariza sat at the kitchen table, doodling in her notebook as she heard Abbu grumble about how much he hated Mondays. He was talking on the phone in the other room, and Pariza could hear him pacing back and forth.

"Mondays are the worst."

"They always seem to last forever, and I still cannot get anything done."

Pariza heard him muttering. He was clearly annoyed.

Pariza smiled to herself and continued drawing. She thought it was funny that Abbu didn't like Mondays. She was drawing a picture of a silly-looking monster with a big grin on its face.

After a while, Abbu hung up the phone and came into the kitchen to check on her. "What are you drawing?" he asked.

"I'm drawing a monster," Pariza said, showing him the picture."

"And it's supposed to be really happy, even though it's a Monday."

Abbu laughed and gave her a hug. "Well, I guess you are right, Parizu. Maybe I should try to be more like you and your Monster and not let the Mondays get me down." Abbu often called her Parizu lovingly.

Pariza grinned and looked up at him. "Abbu, can you teach me how to draw some graphs and data?"

"Of course, Pariza. I'd love to do that," As someone who always wanted his kids to pick data, Abbu was elated with joy.

"The first thing we need for creating a data visualization is data. Why don't you think of some data we can use, and we will meet again after my meeting," Abbu said hopping on to another call with his colleagues.

Time Out!

Data is a collection of relevant and valuable information about something. It can be anything from numbers to words to pictures. For example, if we wanted to know which color of LEGO pieces are most popular, we could count LEGO pieces of each color and write it down. This will be the data of your LEGO pieces which you could use to create graphs to find patterns and make decisions.

A Graph is a simple and effective way to show the data. The Title shows you what you are interpreting. The vertical and the horizontal lines are called axes. The horizontal line is called x-axis and the vertical line is called y-axis.

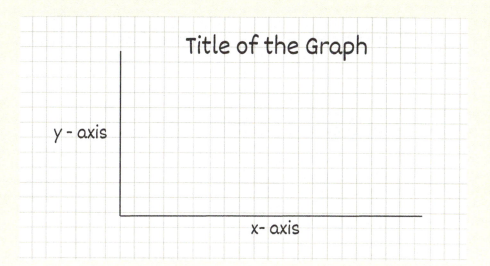

Pariza wondered which data she could use. Some funny ideas came to her mind.

"Maybe I could use the number of chocolate wrappers I've found in Abbu's office or maybe the number of times he lost his socks." Pariza giggled at these thoughts.

She thought of some more ideas, but nothing seemed good enough. Just then she saw the Monster she had drawn in her notebook. She recalled her conversation with Abbu and thought of a brilliant idea. She could use 'days of the week' and 'number of letters' as the data.

Pariza waited eagerly to present her idea to her dad and couldn't wait to see what they drew together with this funny dataset.

A few minutes later, Abbu came and asked, 'Parizu, did you think of a dataset?'

'Yes, Abbu!' Pariza said excitedly and showed him the notebook.

Day of the Week	Number of Letters
MONDAY	6
TUESDAY	7
WEDNESDAY	9
THURSDAY	8
FRIDAY	6
SATURDAY	8
SUNDAY	6

"Hmm, so I see Days of the Week in the first column and Number of letters in the second column. This is wonderful, Pariza," Abbu patted her head.

"Yes, Abbu! And this also has your favorite day," Pariza said teasing Abbu.

"Ha-ha! Yes, I see M O N D A Y has 6 letters."

"Let's begin by drawing a horizontal line, also known as the x-axis," Abbu explained while sketching the line in the notepad. "This is where we'll label the days of the week. Then we'll add a vertical line, also known as the y-axis. From there, we'll place one block for each letter."

"Abbu, for M O N D A Y we will have 6 blocks on top of each other, right?"

"Correct! Here you go."

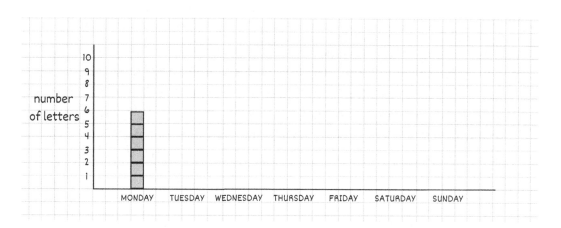

"Now, can you draw for rest of the days?" asked Abbu, handing over the notebook to Pariza.

She added 7 blocks for T U E S D A Y, 9 for W E D N E S D A Y, so on and so forth. Within a few minutes, Pariza completed her first bar-graph.

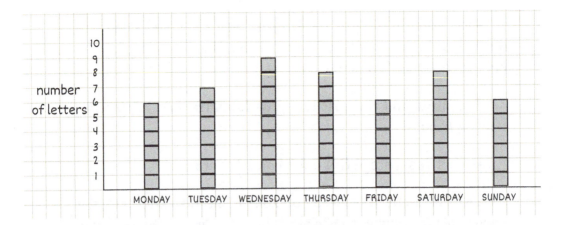

"That, my dear, is a bar graph," Abbu said pointing towards the notebook. Pariza felt a sense of achievement after creating her first bar graph.

Time Out!

A bar graph is like a picture that shows information or data. It has bars of different sizes, and each bar shows a different value. The taller the bar, the greater the value it shows. We use bar graphs to see which values are bigger or smaller, and to see if there are any patterns in the data. The bottom of the bar graph shows the categories we are comparing, and the sides show the values. This makes it easier to compare the data and see what it means.

Another variation of bar graph is called a horizontal bar graph. This type of bar graph is useful for comparing data that has long labels or names, as the labels can be easily read along the horizontal axis. You will see an example of this in Chapter 4 (Ink Sparing Insights).

"Abbu, I see W E D N E S D A Y has the tallest bar," said Pariza pointing at Wednesday in the graph.

"Good observation, Parizu. It has the highest number of letters," responded Abbu.

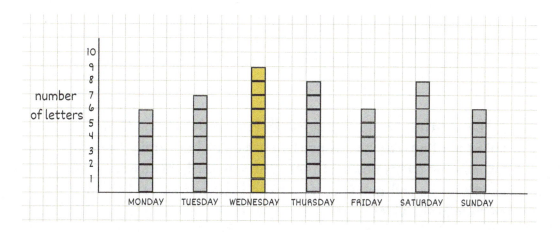

"No wonder I always make mistakes while spelling Wednesday," Pariza giggled.

Your turn to Play

After creating the bar graph with Pariza, Abbu joined his online meeting. Pariza sat next to him on a chair and peeked at his monitor every now and then. She saw that there were five people in the call, and she could read their names next to their picture in the video.

Suddenly, an idea struck her. She thought it would be wonderful to create a bar graph with the names of Abbu's teammates.

She started by creating a table of names and number of letters.

- Complete the table by writing down the number of letters in each name.

Abbu's Friends	Number of Letters
ABDULLAH	
DHRUV	
EIHAB	
OMAR	
SHANGITA	

- Now use the data from the table to create a bar graph you learnt in this chapter.

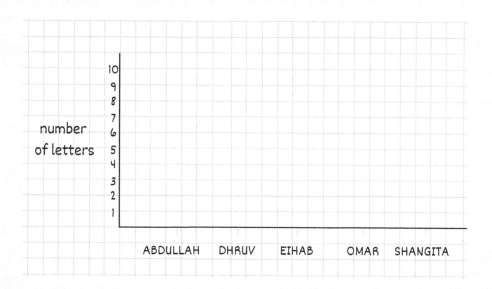

- Examine the graph that you have created and consider its implications. Jot down your observations about the data being presented. Additionally, brainstorm about other similar graphs that you can construct.

03 MONDAY BLUES II

It was 5 pm and Abbu had just wrapped up another office meeting. He grumbled as he walked into the living room.

'I hate Mondays.' He said to himself but then he saw Pariza sitting at the table engrossed in her notebook and a smile spread across his face.

"What are you working on, Parizu? Is that a Monster again?" he asked.

"I'm practicing creating a bar graph," Pariza looked up from her notebook briefly and said "It's so much fun! It's like painting, but with numbers instead of colors."

"I'm glad you like it," Abbu said. "Do you want to try a different type of graph this time? A line graph, maybe?"

"A line-graph?" Pariza asked, her eyes lighting up. "What's that?"

"Remember, the Snore Graph you created showing how the loudness of my snores changed with time?"

"Ha ha! That was funny, Abbu."

Abbu smiled and continued, "A line graph is similar to a bar graph, but instead of bars, it uses lines to show the data," Abbu explained. "It can be a good way to show how the data changes over time or a sequence."

"That sounds awesome! Can we make one together?" Pariza was eager to learn more.

"Of course," Abbu said, taking the notebook from Pariza. "What data should we use?"

"Can we use the 'days of the week' dataset again?" asked Pariza.

"Sure! Let's use the letters of the days of the week and show the trend based on position of the letters," Abbu explained.

He continued as he started drawing in the notebook, "We'll start by labeling the x-axis for position of the letter and on the y-axis, let's write down all the alphabets."

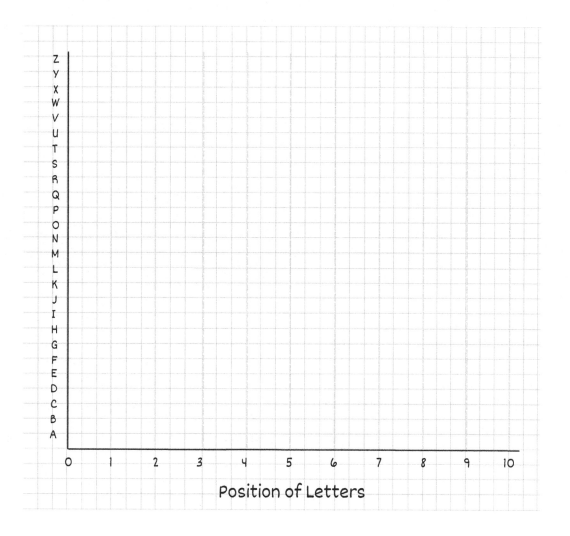

"The first day of the week is M O N D A Y. So, for Monday, M is the first letter, O is the second letter, so on and so forth."

He plotted the letters of the word M O N D A Y in the graph using dots.

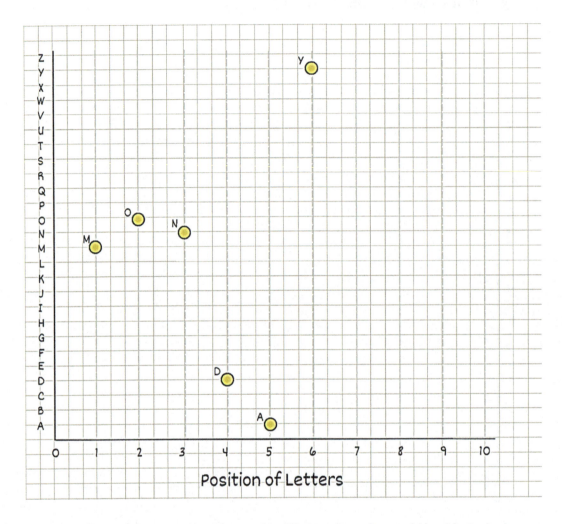

"Abbu, where is the line" asked Pariza as she watched her dad with curiosity.

"Here you go," said Abbu, connecting the dots on the graph.

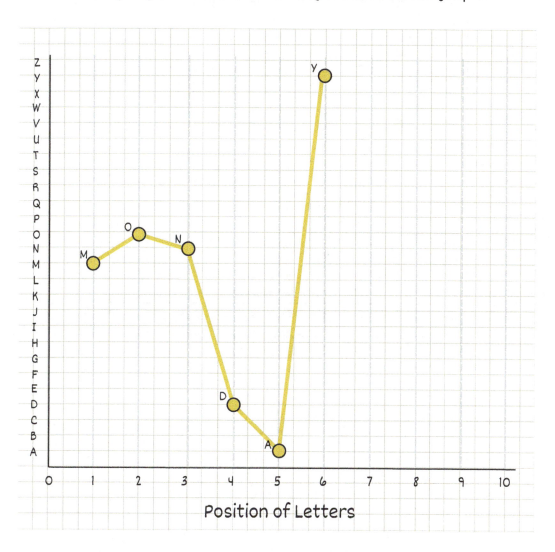

"Oh, this is wonderful!" said Pariza, clapping her hands excitedly.

"Let's add another day here. What's your favorite day?" asked Abbu.

"Sunday. Abbu, let's add S U N D A Y."

Abbu repeated the same exercise for S U N D A Y. First, he drew dots based on the position of the letters. And then he connected them, just like he did for M O N D A Y.

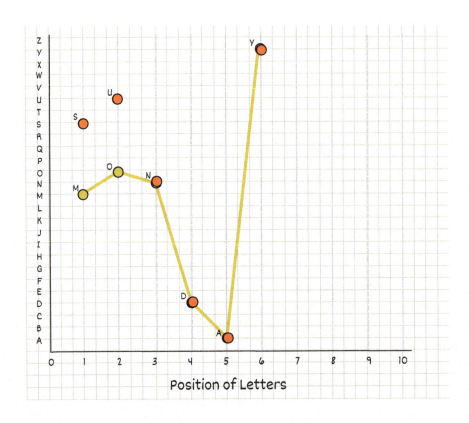

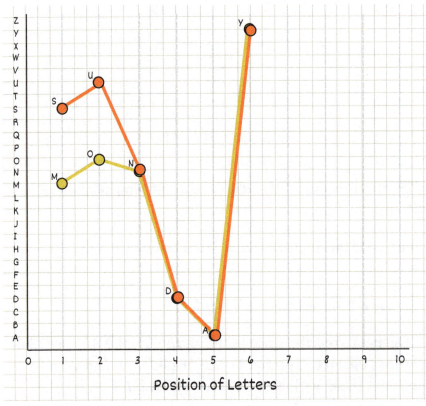

22 | DRAWING DATA WITH KIDS

"There, we're done!" Abbu said, handing over the notebook to Pariza. She looked at it admiringly. She started grinning as she noticed a pattern.

"What happened?" asked Abbu.

"Abbu! Did you observe that M O N D A Y looks so much like

S U N D A Y in the graph?" said Pariza with a big smile.

"Ha-ha! Yes, every day is similar. It depends on how we look at it. I had a wonderful time drawing these graphs with you. I hope you also had a good time."

Pariza was smiling ear to ear as she nodded happily.

Time Out!

Line Graphs are a way of showing how things change over time or in a sequence. They are made up of a line or lines that connects points on a graph. Each point represents a specific time or a sequence and has a value associated with it. For example, if we wanted to show how the temperature changed over a week, we could make a line graph. Each day would be a point on the graph, and the temperature would be the value.

Further we could add more than one line to the graph so we can compare them. For example, we could draw a line graph to compare the temperature of Seattle and San Francisco.

Your turn to Play

After drawing the graph with Pariza, Abbu went back to work. Pariza sat there thinking what she should do next. She tried to read a book, water the plants, talk to Mom but she kept thinking about the line graph that she had drawn with her dad.

She picked up her notebook and started plotting other days of the week. Can you help her with that?

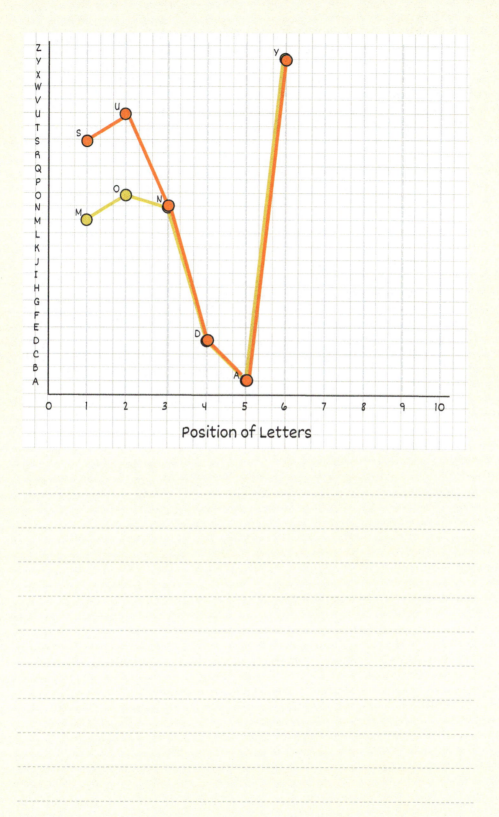

04 INK-SPARING INSIGHTS

The next morning, Pariza woke up to find Abbu getting ready for his morning jog. It was his favorite activity of the day and he always looked forward to it.

In Abbu's words,

"When you go running, you get fresh air in your lungs and fresh ideas in your mind. So, you have a bright mind and a healthy body for the rest of the day."

Pariza wasn't a fan of running. She got innovative ideas while doodling in her notebook.

And she got a brilliant idea about Abbu's running and her newly acquired skill of making graphs. She started drawing something about Abbu's runs...

Abbu jogging in the park

She smiled as she recalled what her mom had said the other day. "You know, Pariza, your dad burns more calories when he goes jogging with you than when he goes by himself."

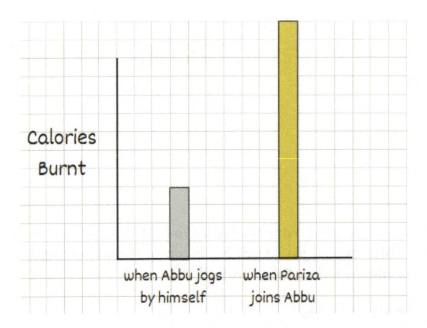

Abbu returned soon after. He saw Pariza sitting at the table engrossed in her notebook. She looked at him and held up her notebook to show him what she had been doing.

"Abbu, look what I have been drawing while you were away."

"Ha ha! This looks really cool but can you do me a favor and write down the date here? Adding dates to your notes makes it more organized. And when I grow old, I'll remember the days when my little girl made these funny doodles."

Pariza took the notebook and started putting dates on her work. As she was writing the date 5th November, her pen ran out of ink.

"Oh no, my pen ran out of ink!" Pariza frowned as she shook the pen, hoping it would start working again.

As she was trying to write November, she said "Abbu, I don't know why they must use so many letters to coin the name of the month

N O V E M B E R. One, Two, Three, Four, Five, six, Seven and Eight, phew! It feels like they were playing scrabble when they came up with the names of the months." She giggled at her amusing thought.

"Ha ha! Great observation, Pariza," Abbu responded, bewildered by her thought. He was also at a loss for words.

Suddenly, he had an idea. "It does look like someone was playing scrabble when they coined these month names. Some months have so many letters and some have very few. Do you want to do some fun data analysis on the spellings of the months?"

Pariza clapped her hands excitedly, "Yes! That sounds great. Can we do it now?"

"Sure thing. Let's grab a pen and some paper and we can get started." Abbu started helping her chalk out the details.

Pariza went straight to preparing data. Like the previous exercise, she created a table with Months and number of characters for each month's name.

Months	Number of Letters
JANUARY	7
FEBRUARY	8
MARCH	5
APRIL	5
MAY	3
JUNE	4
JULY	4
AUGUST	6
SEPTEMBER	9
OCTOBER	7
NOVEMBER	8
DECEMBER	8

She started creating a bar-graph, but she realized that the months' names might overlap. So, she decided to create a horizontal bar-graph she had learnt in the prior lessons.

Time Out!

In Chapter 2, you were introduced to Bar Graphs, in which we constructed a Vertical Bar Graph depicting the number of letters in Days of the Week.

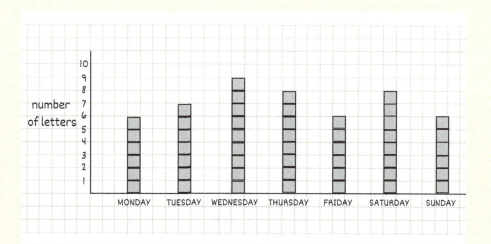

Now, another type of bar graph known as the Horizontal Bar Graph is worth considering. It is particularly helpful when comparing data with long labels or names, as the labels can be read with ease along the horizontal axis. This chapter aims to explore this variation by creating a Horizontal Bar Graph, which may reveal some interesting differences.

Then she created bars for the rest of the months.

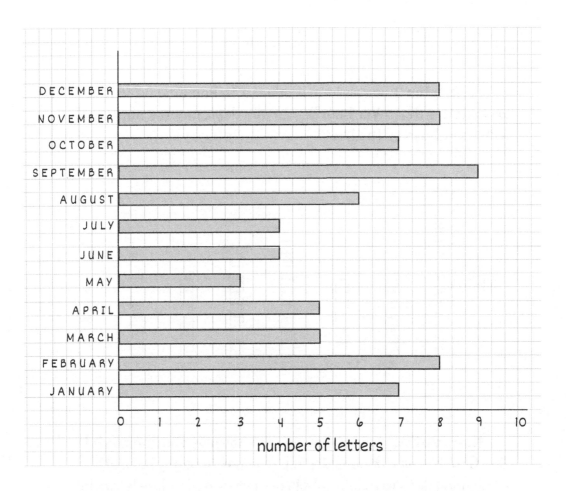

"Wow! This was so much fun, Abbu." Pariza was happy with the outcome. She admired the graph. "This looks like stairs of different lengths."

"Data is always fun. It's like writing a story but with numbers. And looks like you have understood the bar-graphs nicely." Abbu patted her head and appreciated her work. "Now, look at this graph carefully and tell me what you see. Do you notice something?"

Pariza thought for a moment and said, "Abbu, the month of May is the best month. The World would have saved so much ink if all the months were just 3 letters long."

"Ha-ha! Nice observation, Pariza. That's why some of the calendars just use the first 3 letters of each month."

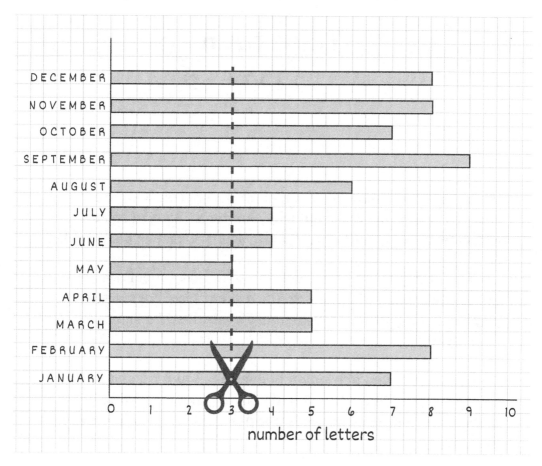

JAN	FEB	MAR	APR
MAY	JUN	JUL	AUG
SEP	OCT	NOV	DEC

Your turn to Play

"Abbu, I'm going to make a graph of all the chocolates you eat while I'm asleep and will send it to your team." Pariza complained after finding yet another chocolate wrapper on her dad's table.

Abbu shrugged his shoulders and said "I am sorry I ate your chocolate again. But I think that's a great idea, Pariza. Why don't you bring your notebook, and we will create a graph of chocolates?"

However, since Pariza didn't have the actual record of the number of chocolates her dad ate so far, they decided to create a bar-chart based on number of letters in the spelling of each chocolate.

After the graph is complete, carefully analyze it and contemplate its implications. Record your observations on what the graph is conveying. Additionally, brainstorm other comparable graphs that you can make.

Chocolate	Number of Letters
SNICKERS	8
KITKAT	6
TWIX	4
TOBLERONE	9
HERSHEYS	8
GODIVA	6
MARS	4

05 SNAKES & LADDERS

Abbu was cleaning up the kitchen when he heard a loud cry from the adjacent room.

"Abbu, Abbu!" Pariza's younger brother came running to the kitchen with tears rolling down his face. Pariza was right behind him.

"Aapi[1] ruined all my LEGO buildings! I spent so much time building them. I'm never going to play with her again. She always does this." He pointed at Pariza and said in one breath.

---

1 "Aapi" is a word in the Urdu language that means "elder sister." It is a term of respect and affection, used to address an older sister or an older woman who is considered a sisterly figure. It is commonly used in South Asia, particularly in Pakistan and India, where Urdu is spoken.

"Abbu, I was just cleaning up the room that Mom asked me to, and his LEGO structures fell by mistake and broke," Pariza said in her defense.

Abbu tried to be the referee for a few minutes. Realizing rebuilding those colorful buildings was the only way to pacify him, Abbu eventually decided to help him rebuild the LEGO[2] structures.

The young gentleman was now happy, with a broad grin on his face, arranging and admiring his newly created real estate.

Even though the younger brother had managed to regain his composure, Pariza was still feeling bad for the fact that he had cried, which she believed was a result of her actions.

She went and sat next to him and asked him to show the new buildings to her. He obliged happily and after he was done boasting about his empire, Pariza gave him a tight hug.

"Aapi, can we please play Snakes & Ladders?" he asked.

Pariza wanted to read the new book she got from the library, but she couldn't say no to her brother. They started playing and Abbu was back in kitchen, helping Pariza's mother with the dishes.

A few minutes into the game they started fighting again. Abbu was done with the dishes by the time. He came and enquired, "What happened my dear kids?"

"Abbu, we were playing, and I was about to win the game when he threw all our pieces on the floor saying this game is not fair and that it has more snakes then ladders." Pariza was furiously

---

[2] At the time of writing this book, there was a massive earthquake in Turkey & Syria where around 60 thousand lives were lost, and thousands of buildings were damaged. It will take years to rebuild the infrastructure and bring back the smile to survivors. Wish it was as simple as rebuilding the LEGO buildings.

complaining about her brother who she had hugged just a few minutes back.

Abbu started laughing as he was thinking to introduce a new data visualization to the kids.

"Well, that's easy thing to check. Parizu, let us count the number of snakes & ladders on this board."

One, two, three, four, five, six, seven and eight". They counted eight ladders and then started counting the number of snakes.

Snakes & Ladders | 39

"One, two, three, four, fix, six, seven and eight," Pariza counted and then continued "See, I told you both snakes and ladders are equal in number." The younger brother was scratching his head and was listening.

Pariza loved doodling. As she was talking, she immediately drew a circle dividing it into two equal parts and explained to the younger brother, "See the left side is the number of Snakes, and the right side is the number of Ladders, and they both are equal."

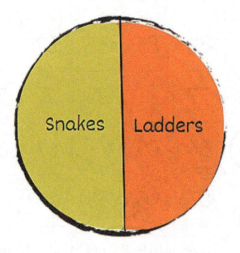

Abbu was surprised and proud at the same time of her visual skills.

"Pariza, do you know you just created a pie chart?"

"Pie chart? Yeah, it does look like a pie with different fillings on both sides," she said and laughed.

"Yeah, a pie chart is one of the most used charts in data visualization. It is a way of showing information in a circle, and each slice represents a different part of the information you want to show."

"Hmm, just like how I showed about the number of snakes & ladders, Abbu?"

'Exactly.'

'Abbu, what if the number of snakes & ladders were different? What if we had 15 snakes and 5 ladders?'

'This is where we will use fractions, Parizu. Do you want to give it a try?' asked Abbu.

Pariza remembered her math class lesson and did a little calculation:

Fraction of Ladders = (Number of Ladders)/ (Number of Ladders + Number of Snakes)

= 5/ (5+15)
= 5/20
= 1/4

'Abbu, I got 1/4th as a fraction.'

'Yes, you would have a quarter of a slice for ladders and the rest of it for snakes.'

'Ok, let me give it a try,' said Pariza and drew a circle. She then created a quarter of the slice for ladders and the rest for snakes.

"Nice, so now you know how to create a pie-chart." Abbu felt happy to see the result.

"Yes, the circular shape makes it more beautiful," Pariza said admiring her newly created visualization.

Time Out

A pie chart is a special kind of graph that looks like a circle, cut into slices. Each slice represents the respective portion. Pie charts are a wonderful way to show how various parts relate to the whole, and they're especially useful when you want to compare the sizes of distinct groups.

Pie charts are not always the best choice, however. If you want to compare more than a few groups, a bar graph might be a better choice. A bar graph uses bars to show the size of each group, and it's easier to compare many groups with a bar graph than with a pie chart.

Your turn to Play

On a hot summer day, Pariza's Mom decided to make a Watermelon Pizza. She wanted to surprise Pariza, who wondered about the sauce and toppings for this new type of pizza.

'It will have Yogurt as sauce and blueberries and strawberries as toppings,' Mom revealed.

Abbu exclaimed, 'Wow, that sounds like my type of healthy pizza.'

After Mom cut the pizza into six equal parts and added the sauce and toppings, Abbu, feeling very hungry, quickly ate three pieces. Meanwhile, Pariza, Mom, and their younger brother each had one slice.

- Pariza wanted to create a pie chart to show who ate how many slices. Can you help her create this visual using a pie chart?

06 SNAKES & LADDERS II

After enjoying the delicious watermelon pizza, Abbu quietly slipped away to his home-office to get some work done. Since becoming a dad, he had mastered the art of treading softly, and opening and closing doors with minimal noise. Afterall, Pariza had been a light sleeper as a baby, and the slightest sound would wake her up, causing her to cry for hours.

Abbu had just opened his laptop when he heard the pattering of footsteps behind him. He turned around to see Pariza and her brother rushing toward him.

Pariza exclaimed, "Abbu, it's a weekend. Please play a board game with us."

Abbu smiled and said, "I need to get some work done, but I can spare some time for a quick game. How about we play Snakes & Ladders?"

The younger brother groaned, "But I always get more snakes than everyone else! It's not fair."

Pariza giggled, "Maybe you have a snake magnet in your pocket."

Everyone laughed, and Abbu suggested they count the number of snakes and ladders each person encounters during the game. He was already imagining the kind of graph he would create with this data.

As they played, the game quickly turned interesting, with each player hopping between ladders and snakes. The younger brother, who had been worried about his snake streak, began to move ahead faster. To everyone's surprise, he emerged as the winner of the game!

He jumped up and down with joy. Pariza looked at Abbu and shrugged. Abbu was more interested in the data and Pariza peeked over his shoulder.

Player	Number of Snakes	Number of Ladders
Pariza	4	2
Brother	2	4
Mom	2	2
Abbu	4	1

"Abbu, what are we going to do with this data?"

"This is interesting data, Parizu. We can use this to create a Scatter Plot and see who encountered more snakes or ladders."

"Scatter Plot?" Pariza asked with her eyes wide open.

Abbu smiled and explained, "A scatter plot is a graph that shows the relationship between two sets of data. We can plot the number of snakes on one axis and the number of ladders on the other axis. This way, we can visualize who got more snakes or ladders and how they affect the game's outcome."

Time Out!

A scatter plot is a type of graph that shows the relationship between two different sets of data. It's called a scatter plot because the data points are plotted on the graph like a bunch of scattered dots.

Pariza watched closely as Abbu plotted the data on a notebook. He drew a horizontal line and labeled it as "Number of Snakes" and a vertical line labeled as "Number of Ladders."

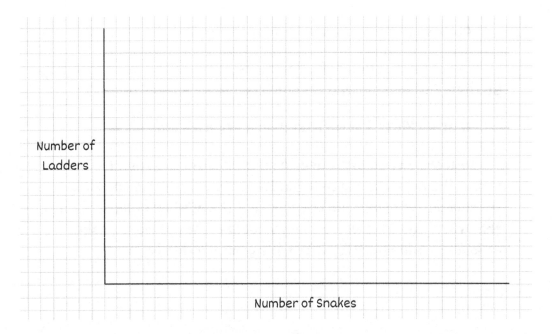

"This is a very interesting, Parizu. Watch closely," Abbu said as he created a vertical line that cut the graph into two equal portions.

"Since the number of Snakes as we go from left to right increases, we'll have less Snakes on left side of the graph and more on the right side." Abbu explained.

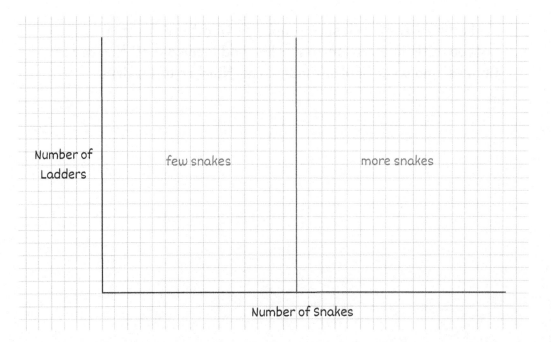

Pariza scratched her head and asked, "What about the Ladders, Abbu?"

"Yes," he said and created another graph. This time he created a horizontal line to cut the graph in two equal portions horizontally. "As the number of Ladders increases from bottom to top, we will have less ladders at the bottom and more on the top."

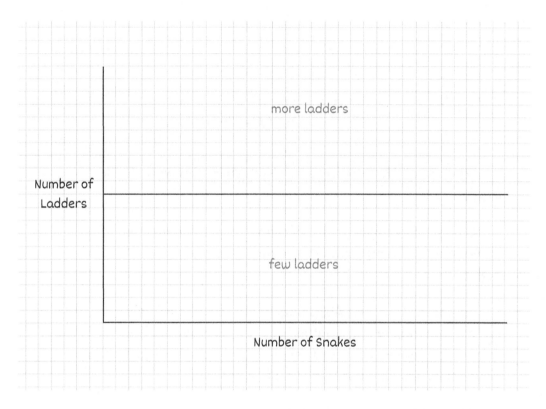

Pariza was listening patiently and then asked, "Abbu, why did you create two different graphs?"

"That's just to explain to you, Pariza. Check this out," he said creating a third graph. This time he cut the graph in four equal portions by a vertical and a horizontal line."

```
                  |
  few snakes      |   more snakes
  more ladders    |   more ladders
                  |
Number of ————————+————————————————
Ladders           |
  few snakes      |   more snakes
  few ladders     |   few ladders
                  |
         Number of Snakes
```

Pariza was thoroughly confused. "Abbu, can you please explain this?"

Abbu happily obliged, "So, we want to put the number of snakes and ladders each person got in our game on this graph, right?"

Pariza nodded, and Abbu continued, "On the left side, you will have lesser number of snakes, and as you move to the right, the number of snakes will increase. Similarly, the bottom half will have fewer ladders compared to the top half."

"Abbu, these look like four rooms of a house."

"You are right, Pariza. I didn't think of that. Which room would you like to be to win the game?"

"Abbu, I don't like Snakes. I want to be the top left room with few snakes & more ladders."

"Good choice! Let's now put our scores in the graph."

Pariza helped Abbu put the scores in the graph one after the other.

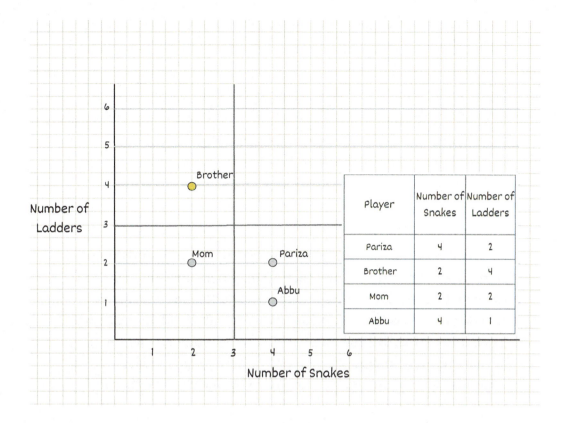

Pariza looked at the graph closely and giggled, "Abbu, look, we both are in the same room. Ha ha! We had so many snakes hissing at us."

Abbu chuckled, "Yes, and if you look closely, your brother won because he had few snakes and more ladders, so he was able to reach the finishing point faster."

Pariza exclaimed, "Abbu, I really like this graph."

Your turn to Play

Excited about her newfound knowledge of scatter plots, Pariza challenged her younger brother to another game of Snakes & Ladders. After an intense match, they both recorded their final scores. Now it is your turn to try your hand at creating a scatter plot with their scores. Use what you have learned in this chapter to plot the number of snakes and ladders encountered by each player and see who emerges as the winner.

Are you up for the challenge?

Player	Number of Snakes	Number of Ladders
Pariza	6	8
Brother	12	4
Mom	8	6
Abbu	10	5

Number of Ladders

Number of Snakes

07 PARATHA[3] PATTERNS

It was eight am on a Sunday morning. Pariza woke up and went straight to the kitchen. She saw Abbu flipping through a cookbook with a determined look on his face. She looked at him quizzically for a moment. He was engrossed in his book.

Pariza said in a pleading voice, 'Abbu, I'm starving! Can you make some Parathas for breakfast?

I miss the Parathas Dadi* used to make when we visited India."

Abbu looked up from the cookbook and chuckled.

"Sure thing, Pariza. What shape paratha do you want?"

---

[3] Paratha is a flaky layered flatbread usually made from whole wheat flour and cooked in butter. It is popular in South Asian region and many varieties of Parathas are found in countries like India, Pakistan, Bangladesh, Sri Lanka, and Nepal.

Pariza asked with raised eyebrows,
"Shape? I didn't know parathas come in different shapes."

Abbu chuckled again and explained,
"Oh yes, Parizu! You can make parathas in all sorts of shapes and sizes. Wait, let me show you some magic with parathas."

With that, Abbu got to work on his first paratha. He took a ball of dough and began rolling it out on the countertop, using a rolling pin. Soon, a square shaped paratha was ready.

Pariza was bemused. "Whoa, that looks cool! Can I make the next one please?"

Abbu nodded and handed over the rolling pin to Pariza "Of course, Parizu. Here you go." He stood there supervising.

Pariza took the dough and began rolling out her first paratha. She took a pause, looked at the soon-to-be-made paratha and exclaimed.

"This is so much fun. I'm also going to make a square paratha."

"Go for it. I'll make a rectangle." Abbu encouraged her as he picked up another rolling pin and started rolling out another paratha.

Pariza imitated Abbu and soon her Paratha was ready. She looked at it confidently and waited for Abbu's reaction.

Abbu smiled at Pariza and patted her head. "Very nice, Pariza, but this is looking more like a Parallelogram."

"Ha-ha, yes! It does look like a Parallelogram." Pariza chuckled as she realized that the paratha looked more like a parallelogram than a square.

"Abbu, I wonder how they come up with such names. SQUARE, RECTANGLE and PARALLELOGRAMS, all have 4 four sides but the number of letters in each word are so different."

"Hmmm! Good observation. We should do a little data visualization for the shapes and their spellings. What say?" Abbu was also done rolling his rectangle-shaped paratha.

Pariza was excited at the thought of learning a new data visualization concept. "That sounds like fun, Abbu, but first let's finish breakfast. I am very hungry."

As the parathas sizzled on the hot pan, Pariza and Abbu shared a laugh and enjoyed the multi-shaped creations.

After the breakfast, Pariza brought her notebook to the dining table and eagerly waited for instructions from Abbu.

"Abbu! How do we start?"

Abbu came and sat near Pariza as he wiped his hands dry. "We will start the same way we did for our previous graph. First, write down the name of the shapes, add the number of sides in one column, and number of characters in the other."

Pariza started immediately. "And then I can create a scatterplot again!"

"Exactly!" Abbu said.

Shape	Sides	Letters
TRIANGLE	3	8
SQUARE	4	6
RECTANGLE	4	9
PARALELOGRAM	4	12
PENTAGON	5	8
HEXAGON	6	7
SEPTAGON	7	8
OCTAGON	8	7

"Okay, so we have the data now. What do I do next?" Pariza asked Abbu after she finished making the data table.

"Pariza, do you remember whether the x-axis is the horizontal or the vertical line?"

Pariza said, "Of course, x-axis is horizontal! I used to get confused earlier but I have a way to remember it. I think of it as the swords of two people fighting on a horizontal plane."

"Ha-ha! That's a clever way to remember I guess." Abbu was amused at Pariza's thought process.

Pariza asked looking at the graph, "Abbu, what do we do next?"

Abbu gave her further instructions, "Now, create an x-axis and a y-axis and then start adding the data points."

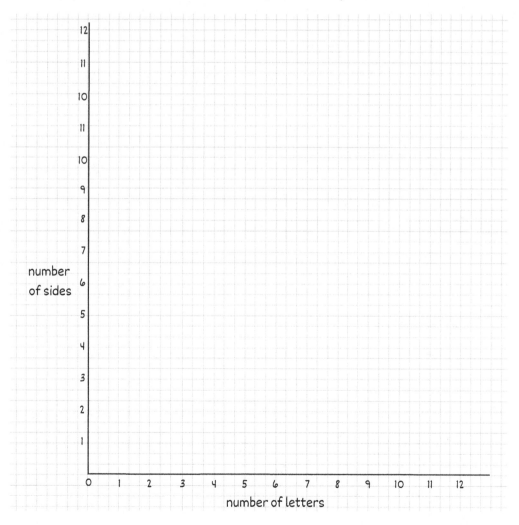

Pariza soon finished drawing the x-axis for 'number of letters' and the y-axis for 'number of sides'.

Then she started adding the data points.

'First, let me plot a SQUARE.'

Abbu was monitoring her closely, 'Ok, check the table for its coordinates.'

Pariza looked at the table and said, 'SQUARE has 4 sides and 6 letters so the coordinates will be (4,6)'

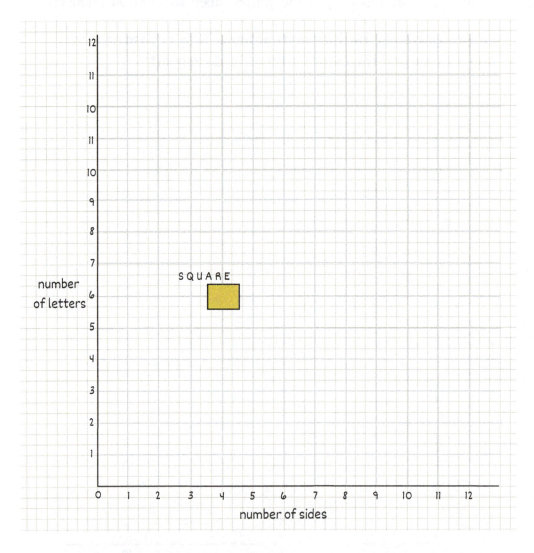

She looked at Abbu for approval.

"Ah, I see you have created the square instead of just marking the coordinate. Very smart of you."

"Yes Abbu, I thought why not just put the shape itself instead of just a dot. Does that work?" she asked inquisitively.

"It does and it is wonderful." Abbu smiled.

She continued to add other shapes on the graph.

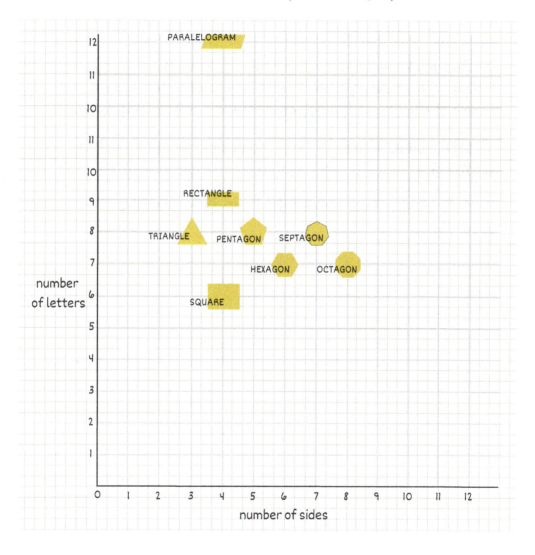

"Here you go! Presenting to you the scatter plot of different shapes inspired by Abbu's creative parathas." Pariza proudly held up her notebook to show Abbu her scatterplot.

Paratha Patterns | 61

Abbu said, "Very cool. You are a scatter plot pro. Now, tell me, do you see anything interesting here?"

Pariza looked at her graph again and thought, "Ummm let me see..."

"Abbu, Square, Rectangle and Parallelograms all have same number of sides, yet it is so easy to spell Square as opposed to parallelogram. I love Squares."

"Ha ha!," Abbu laughed.

"And you know what?" she continued, "Abbu, the way you were telling me to draw a graph, it felt like you were telling me a recipe of some sort." Pariza chuckled at her own imagination.

Abbu laughed and said, "Isn't it a recipe? Recipe to make a scatterplot."

Both laughed heartily at little Pariza's interesting observation.

Your turn to Play

You saw how Pariza had two columns in her data and plotted that in a graph. It's your turn to create a Scatter plot now. Complete the table below by counting the number of Consonants and number of Vowels for each shape.

Shape	Consonants	Vowels
TRIANGLE		
SQUARE		
RECTANGLE		
PARALELOGRAM		
PENTAGON		
HEXAGON		
SEPTAGON		
OCTAGON		

Now, using the data from the table above, create a scatter plot below.

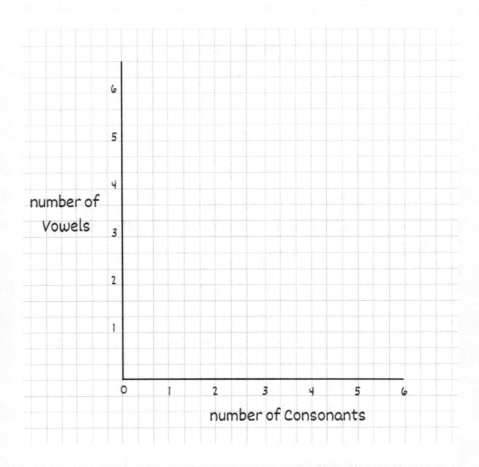

Examine the graph that you have created and consider its implications. Jot down your observations about the data being presented. Additionally, brainstorm about other similar graphs that you can construct.

----

08 BOARD GAME NIGHT

It was five past seven in the evening and Pariza was sitting at the kitchen table. Her eyebrows furrowed in disappointment as she stared at the Scrabble board in front of her.

Her best friend Priya had just left. And although Pariza had fun playing board games with her, she was now disappointed because she had lost the last game of scrabble against Priya.

Abbu walked in and noticed Pariza frowning, "What's the matter, Parizu? How was the game with Priya? Did you have an enjoyable time?"

Pariza said, sighing heavily, "Yes, we had a great time, but I lost the game and it's so frustrating."

Her dad chuckled and placed a comforting hand on her shoulder.

"Don't worry about winning or losing, Parizu. It's okay to experience both. Winning and losing are natural parts of the game."

Pariza nodded, but still looked unconvinced. Abbu noticed her disappointment and came up with an idea to cheer her up.

"Hey, I have an idea," he said with a mischievous twinkle in his eyes. "Why don't we make a little data visualization to analyze what happened in the game? That way we can see if there are any patterns."

Being a data nerd, he wouldn't let go of any opportunity to bring data visualization into the conversation.

Pariza's face lit up at the thought. She loved working with numbers and data, and the idea of creating a graph of her latest game with Priya sounded like a lot of fun.

"Yes! Let's do it!" she exclaimed, instantly forgetting the disappointment of the game.

Abbu smiled and said, "Alright! Bring your scorebook and we will get started right away."

Pariza ran to fetch her scorebook and quickly created the table below.

Round	Pariza	Priya
1	14	15
2	10	8
3	16	4
4	7	9
5	11	11
6	22	37
Total	80 ☹	84

Abbu looked at the scores and said, "Wow! This looks like a close game."

Pariza said, "Yes! That's why it is more disappointing. I was so close to winning. Abbu, should I create a bar-graph?"

"It depends on what question you want to answer with the graph, Pariza."

Pariza was a little confused, "What do you mean, Abbu?"

"Each graph type we use in analyzing data has a specific use-case. If you want to understand how you did in each round, you could use a bar-graph. However, if you want to see how the running total[4] changed with each round we could use a line-graph."

---

4 The running total allows you to see the sum-total of all the values up to a certain point in time, rather than just looking at the individual values themselves. This can be helpful for tracking progress or analyzing trends over time. But don't worry about this now. We will cover this more in the next chapter.

Pariza was listening intently, 'That's interesting. How about we start with a bar-graph first?'

Abbu nodded and said, 'That's a good choice. However, this is different from the bar graph you created earlier.'

'How?' Pariza asked inquisitively.

'Well, this time you need to plot two bars for each round – one for Priya and one for you. So, you might want to use distinct colors to distinguish the bars for the two of you.'

Pariza started plotting the graph, 'Ok, we played 6 rounds so I'll create 6 bars for each of us.'

Pariza started by creating an x-axis for the 'number of rounds'.

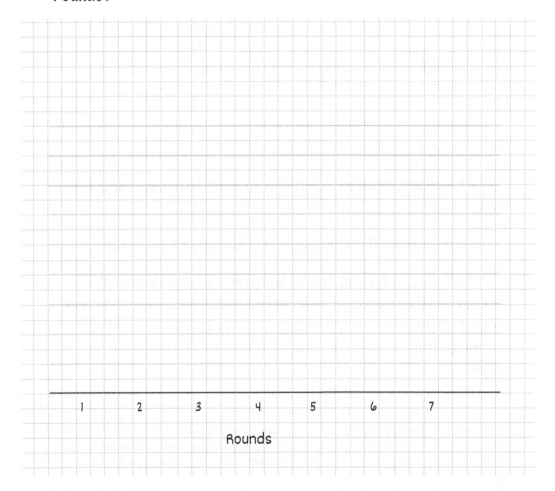

Then she added the y-axis with the score as the vertical line of the graph.

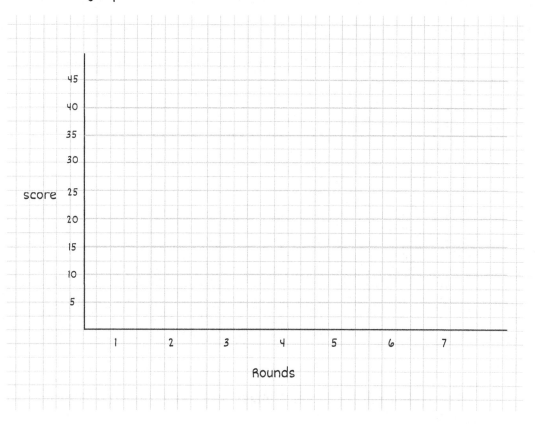

She then plotted the bars for the first round of the game.

Round	Pariza	Priya
1	14	15

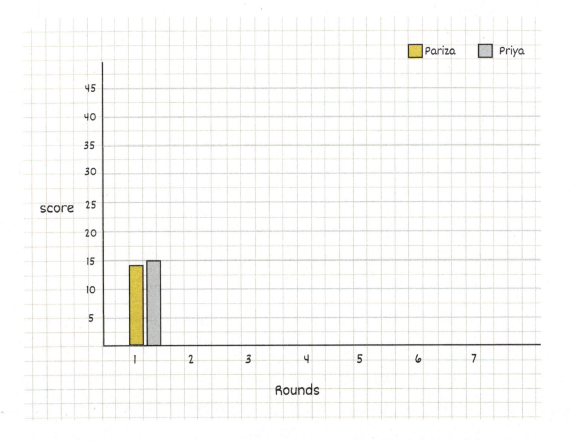

Pariza showed the graph to Abbu and asked, "Abbu, how does this look?"

Abbu nodded in approval and said, "Keep going. This is fascinating! First round was almost equal."

She then added other bars one after the other for each round of the game.

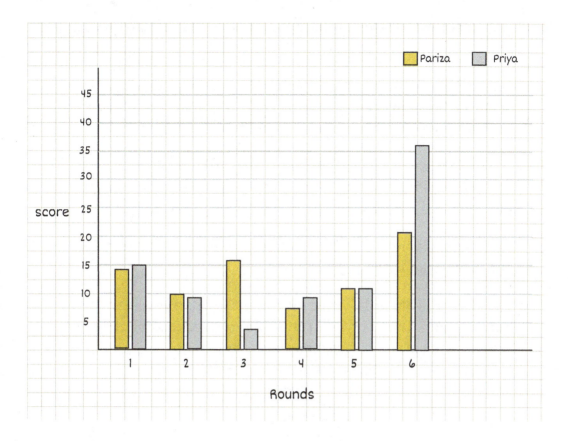

When Pariza finished the graph, she sat back and gazed at it for a moment. A proud smile spread across her face. She showed it to Abbu and waited for his reaction. Abbu looked at the graph carefully and slowly a smile spread on his face too. He was happy with what he saw. Pariza felt proud of herself.

"Great job, Pariza!" he exclaimed, giving her a pat on the back.

"This looks fantastic. You can clearly see how each word contributed to your score. And the colors are a nice touch too."

Pariza beamed at the praise and felt a sense of accomplishment.

She thanked Abbu, "Thanks Abbu! Now, I can see it was a mixed result for most of the game but in the last round she got a Triple Word tile and scored higher."

'Yes! The triple/double words can make a lot of difference in the outcome.'

Pariza continued, 'Abbu, I noticed that this graph shows score of the individual rounds but doesn't tell how much I should have scored in the final round to win the game.'

Abbu smiled and said, 'Good observation, Parizu! I'm so happy you are thinking this way. What you now need is a different type of graph. A line-graph.'

'A line-graph?' asked Pariza inquisitively, getting ready for another visualization.

'Yes, my little Data Detective,' he said with a grin. 'But before that I think it's time for a little break. How about we get some fruits before we solve any more mysteries?'

Pariza giggled and followed her dad to the kitchen. The apples and the bananas helped her feel rejuvenated. She was glad Abbu suggested a break.

(Are you wondering what happened next? Check out the next chapter. But before you go, complete the exercise given below.)

Your turn to Play

One sunny Saturday afternoon, Sara came over to spend some time with Pariza. They played a few games of badminton and tag in the backyard before deciding to head inside to cool off. As they searched for something fun to do, Pariza suggested playing a game of Scrabble. As they played, they laughed, chatted, and had a fun time. Here's the score of their game.

Round	Pariza	Sara
1	8	12
2	8	3
3	17	14
4	21	29
5	15	11
6	31	18

Once the game was over, Pariza wanted to show her data visualization skills to Sara, so she started creating the bar graph with the score data. Can you help Pariza with that?

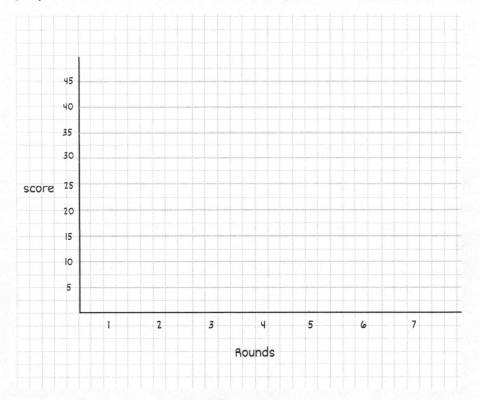

Examine the graph that you have created and consider its implications. Jot down your observations about the data being presented. Additionally, brainstorm about other similar graphs that you can construct.

----

09 BOARD GAME NIGHT II

Pariza felt energized after the snack break, and she was eager to go back to the data visualization activity.

"Abbu, shall I start putting these points in a line-graph," asked Pariza excitedly.

Abbu joined her, "Hang on, dear. We would need to add a couple of columns here, so that we are able to calculate a running total."

"What's a running total, Abbu?" Pariza was confused.

Abbu smiled and said, "Well, imagine this, Parizu. There's a man who is running a race, and after every lap, he gets some mangoes as a reward."

'Wow! I love this race. I love mangoes. So, what happens next?' The thought of winning mangoes in a race amused Pariza.

Abbu chuckles and continues 'After the first lap, he gets 1 mango. After the second, he gets 1 more mango. After the third lap, he gets 3 mangoes. And so on. Even though the number of mangoes he gets after each lap is different, he still wants to keep track of total number of mangoes he is carrying.'

Pariza got thinking and started calculating the number of mangoes on her fingers, 'So after the first lap he has 1 mango, after the second lap he has 1+1 = 2 mangoes and after the third lap he has 2+3 = 5 mangoes.'

'Excellent! This is what a running total is.' Abbu explained. Let us try to jot down the running total for You and Priya now.

Here's the original score that they had jotted earlier:

Round	Pariza	Priya
1	14	15
2	10	8
3	16	4
4	7	9
5	11	11
6	22	37
Total	80 ☹	84

Pariza and Abbu then updated the table by adding the running total score for Pariza.

Round	Pariza	Pariza (Running Total)	Priya	Priya (Running Total)
1	14	14	15	
2	10	24	8	
3	16	40	4	
4	7	47	9	
5	11	58	11	
6	22	80	37	

Then they did the same thing for Priya's score:

Round	Pariza	Pariza (Running Total)	Priya	Priya (Running Total)
1	14	14	15	15
2	10	24	8	23
3	16	40	4	27
4	7	47	9	36
5	11	58	11	47
6	22	80	37	84

Once the table was completed, Abbu said, "Alright! Now we have these 2 extra columns that we would be adding in the line-graph."

It was slightly difficult for Pariza to comprehend this. She asked, "Okay, Abbu. So, we will not be using the actual score but the running total."

"That's right, sweetie pie! We are doing this to see how the two of you were trending after each round. This is similar to what you did for the bar-chart, you can put the rounds in x-axis and on the y-axis, instead of your scores you will put the running totals."

Pariza first drew a horizontal line for Rounds and then a vertical line for the running total.

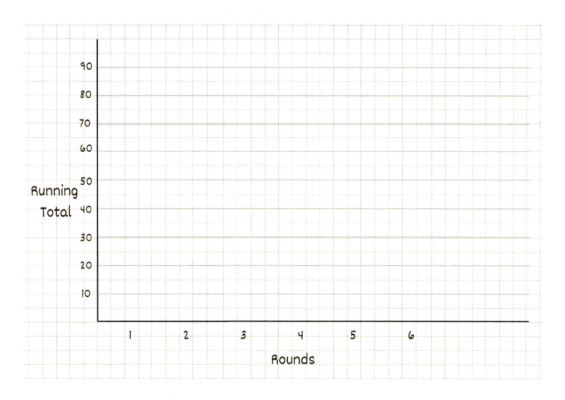

Then she started adding the data points.

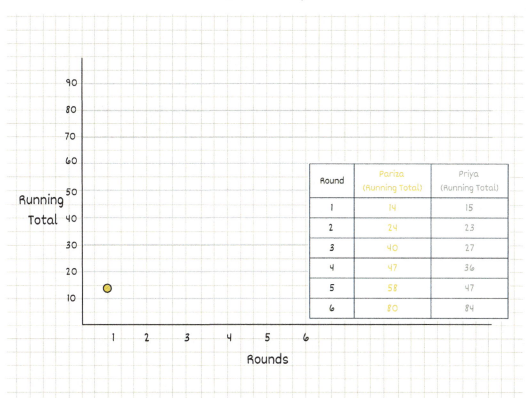

Round	Pariza (Running Total)	Priya (Running Total)
1	14	15
2	24	23
3	40	27
4	47	36
5	58	47
6	80	84

Next, she completed plotting the different points for her running total.

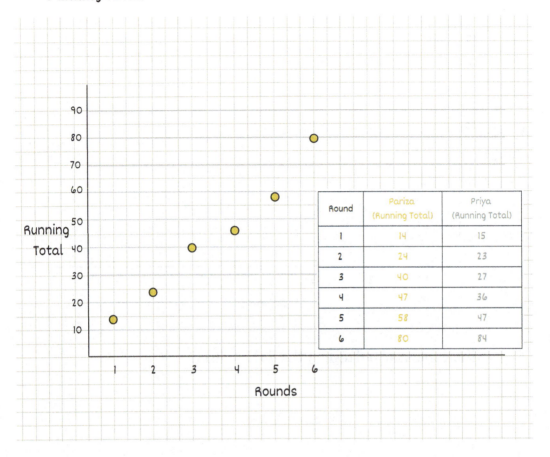

Round	Pariza (Running Total)	Priya (Running Total)
1	14	15
2	24	23
3	40	27
4	47	36
5	58	47
6	80	84

Pariza was happy with what she saw. "Abbu, this is starting to look like the growth chart the doctor shows in every visit. Do I connect these dots now?"

"Ha-ha! Yes, I was thinking the same. Go ahead and connect these dots," Abbu said and waited for her to finish.

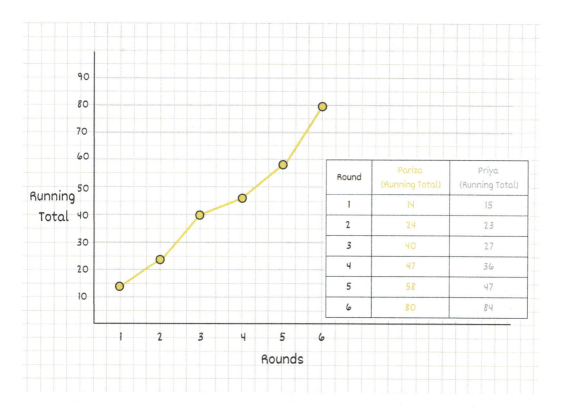

Once she was done connecting the dots, Abbu said, "Excellent! Do you notice anything interesting in this graph, Pariza?"

Pariza thought for a minute and said, "Abbu, the line between Round 3 and Round 4 is less steep."

"Yes, that's right. Now, check the score for these two rounds. You will observe that your score increased just by 7 points in Round 4.

And I agree with you, this does look like the growth-chart we used to see during the pediatrician visit. Your mom used to be so worried with the slightest dip in your weight."

"My Mommy is the best!" Pariza beamed.

"Certainly! Now, do you want to repeat the exercise for Priya's score?"

"Yes! I cannot wait to see how it looks."

Board Game Night II | 81

Firstly, she added the dots for Priya's score on the graph. Then she connected the dots with the lines, just like she had done for her score.

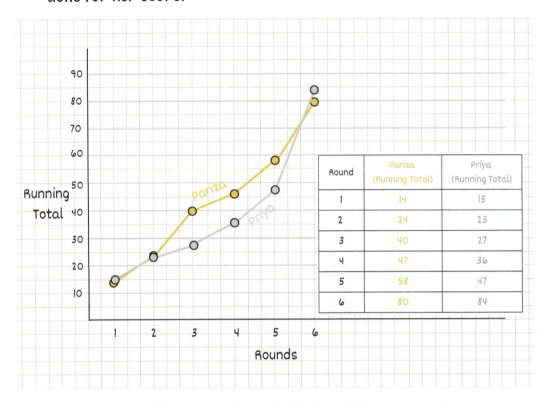

"Oh my God! I was leading all the way, Abbu," Pariza exclaimed with surprise and stood there with her mouth wide open.

"Yes! You were clearly winning for most part of the game and lost with an exceedingly small margin in the end."

"Priya made the letter EQUIP in the last round and got 3 times the points because of the Triple point tile." Pariza analyzed what had made Priya overtake her in the last round.

"So, you now know that you need to target those in the next game." Abbu helped her.

"Abbu, I love how with this graph I could just paint the story of what happened. I wish I could do this all my life."

Your turn to Play

It was another weekend and Priya had come to play with Pariza. They had another game of Scrabble. While Pariza's Dad was talking to Priya's Dad, he was keen to see how Pariza did in this game. He asked Pariza to make a scorecard of the game.

Here's the scorecard. Can you help Pariza create a line-graph to analyze the game?

(Hint: You will need to first help her create additional columns showing the running total of both the players.)

Round	Pariza	Pariza (Running Total)	Priya	Priya (Running Total)
1	22		14	
2	7		14	
3	15		7	
4	10		15	
5	16		16	
6	12		17	

Now use this data to create a line graph to compare Pariza and Priya's scores.

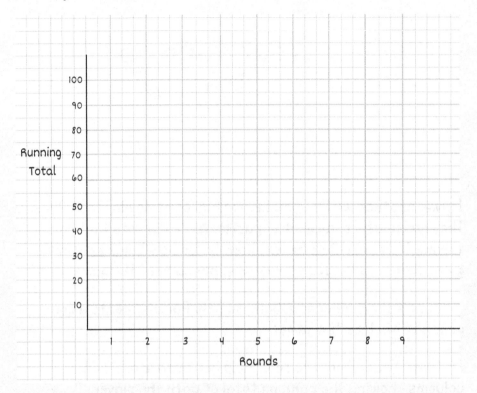

Examine the graph that you have created and consider its implications. Jot down your observations about the data being presented. Additionally, brainstorm other similar graphs that you can construct.

10 SCRABBLE INSIGHTS

It was a rainy Sunday morning and Pariza was a little disappointed that she couldn't go outside and play.

'I wish it stops raining now,' she grumbled, staring out of the window at the gray sky, 'I want to go play at the park today. Rain-rain go away, come back another day...'

Abbu was engrossed in his newspaper. He looked up and saw Pariza's sullen face. That made him put down his newspaper. He came and stood near her. He patted her on the head lovingly and said,

"It's okay, Pariza. Rain is essential for the environment. It helps the plants grow and keep everything healthy."

Pariza considered the thought for a moment. She was split between having a fun time outside and appreciating the importance of rain.

"I guess you are right, Abbu," she said reluctantly. "But it's a Sunday and we were supposed to go out and have fun. Now what are we supposed to do all day?"

Abbu thought for a moment and said, "Well, I have an idea. How about we play Scrabble as a family? Later, we can even use the score for another data visualization exercise like what we did for your game with - Priya."

Pariza's eyes lit up. "That's a great idea! Can we, Mom?" she asked, turning to her mom, who was reading a book.

"Sure, why not? I could use a little brain exercise on a day like this." Her mom put away the book and smiled.

Pariza's younger brother, who had been quietly playing with his toy cars on the floor, looked up at the mention of Scrabble. "Me too! Me too!" he shouted, clapping his hands.

Happy with everyone's response, Pariza ran to her room to retrieve the Scrabble board.

"Okay, let's get started!" she exclaimed, setting the board up on the dining table. Everyone gathered around the table and took their seats.

As they began to play, Pariza made sure to record all the scores carefully and keep track of which words each player had played. She was determined to create the most accurate and informative data story possible.

Round	Pariza	Abbu	Mom	Brother
1	14	22	9	6
2	14	7	6	14
3	7	15	7	9
4	15	10	14	10
5	16	26	14	12
6	21	8	18	14
7	8	21	14	39
8	3	5	12	8
9	15	2	8	6

"It was fun! We ended up using all the letter tiles." Pariza's mom said. They had run out of tiles.

"Yeah! I think it was neck-to-neck. Pariza, do you want to sum up the scores and see who won the game?"

"Abbu, I think it would be fun to do the running total instead. That way I can create a graph as well."

"Sure, that sounds like a good idea." Abbu agreed.

Pariza's younger brother was pleased with his efforts. "I'm sure I'm the winner." He announced gleefully.

Pariza took the score sheet and spent a few minutes creating a new table with the running total. She also used distinct colors for each player.

Round	Pariza	Abbu	Mom	Brother
1	14	22	9	6
2	28	29	15	20
3	35	44	22	29
4	50	54	36	39
5	66	80	50	51
6	87	88	68	65
7	95	109	82	104
8	98	114	94	112
9	113	116	102	118

After she was done creating the table, she looked at the scores for a while. She was a little disappointed to see that her younger brother was the winner. The sibling rivalry made her feel a little jealous.

"Yay!! I'm the best," her younger brother shouted, running around the house and teasing Pariza.

Pariza sighed and looked up at her dad. He was looking at the scoresheet and didn't see the sullen look on Pariza's face. "Hey! Looks like you had a close competition with Mom for the 4th position," he chuckled and spoke. Just then he saw Pariza's face and felt bad for her immediately.

He tried to cheer her up. "Parizu, it was a close game and I think if you draw a graph for it, we might unveil interesting insights."

Pariza perked up at the idea of creating a graph and started creating a line-graph with the scores. Abbu sat down next to her and offered some tips and suggestions, while Pariza worked on her line graph intently.

She started by creating the x-axis for the 'number of rounds' and the y-axis as the running total for each player.

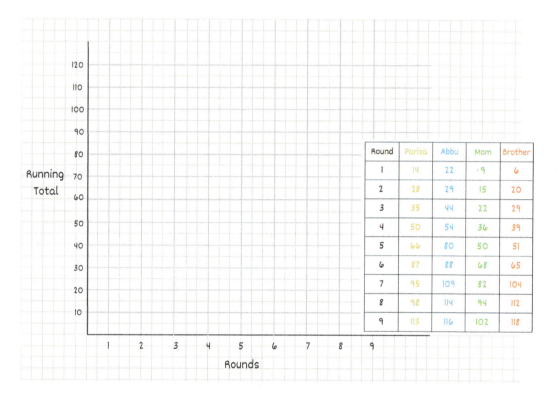

Round	Pariza	Abbu	Mom	Brother
1	14	22	9	6
2	28	29	15	20
3	35	44	22	29
4	50	54	36	39
5	66	80	50	51
6	87	88	68	65
7	95	109	82	104
8	98	114	94	112
9	113	116	102	118

Then she started adding dots for her score and connected them to form a line graph of her score.

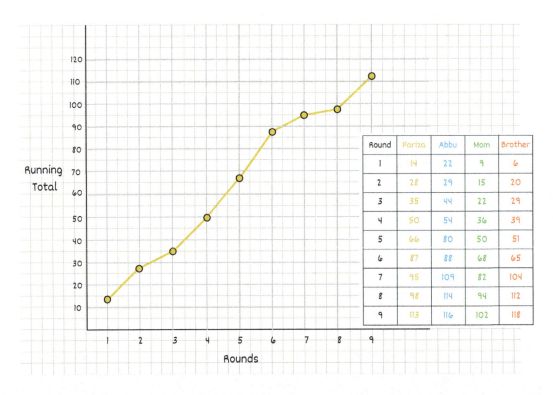

Next, she did the same for Abbu's score. Abbu was sitting tight keen to see what comes next. Secretly, he was also feeling happy and proud to see Pariza doing this analysis by herself.

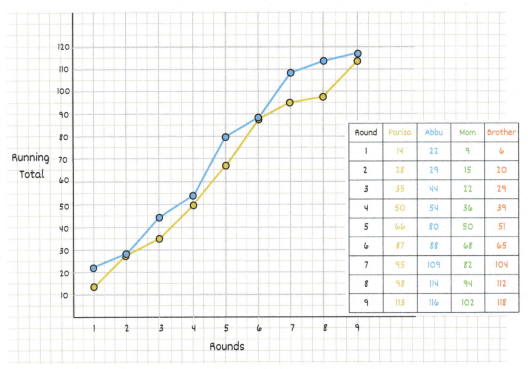

"Abbu, look! You were a little ahead of me for most of the rounds, but I almost touched you at the end." Then she continued to do the same for Mom.

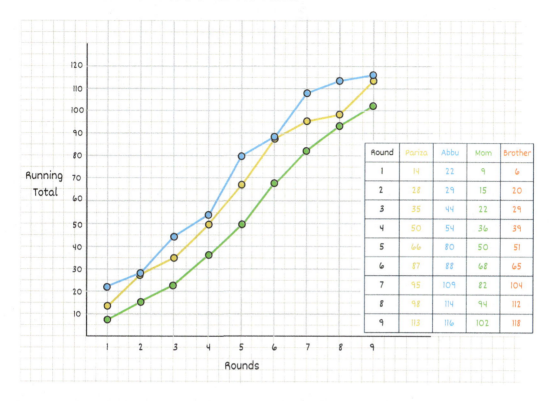

"Abbu, Mom didn't get very good tiles this time. She had very few vowels."

"Yes, I think she still did pretty well," he responded looking at the graph.

Finally, everyone was waiting for younger brother's line to be added in the graph.

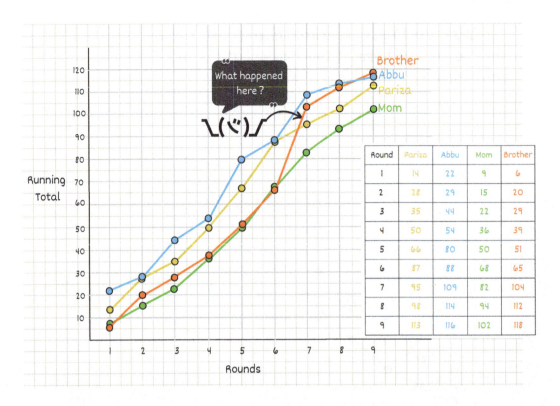

Pariza analyzed the graph and said, "Abbu, round 7 is what made all the difference." She continued to ponder over the graph and the scores while the younger brother kept running all over the house to celebrate his victory.

Your turn to Play

Let's mix things up a bit in this exercise. How about you bring your own data from a game you played with your family or friends?

- Note down the score here

Once you have the scores, use the table below to see if you would want to calculate the Running Total for each player.

- Next you create the line-graph for each player and note down your observations.

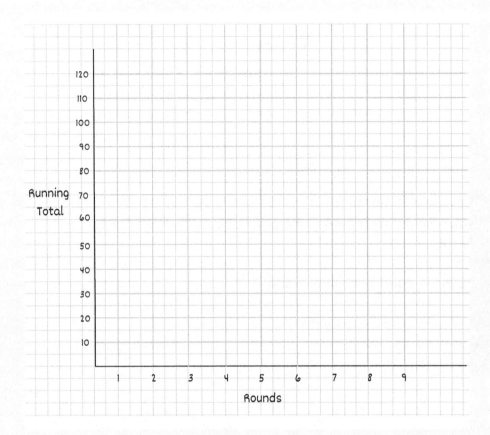

Take a close look at the graph you made and think about what it's telling you. Then write down your thoughts about what the graph is showing.

HEATMAP ON A RAINY DAY

IT had been raining incessantly for one week now. The constant pitter-patter of raindrops had become a monotonous background noise. Pariza was thoroughly frustrated by now. She was starting to feel trapped, unable to go out and enjoy her favorite outdoor activities.

She decided to talk to Abbu, hoping he could help her come up with something fun to do. As she approached him, she noticed that he was looking at his laptop screen intently. "What are you doing, Abbu?" she asked gently.

The question broke his trance. He looked at Pariza and said, "Oh, I am just looking at some weather data. It seems like it's raining everywhere, but it's worse at some places."

Abbu glanced at the screen again and soon became engrossed in it. Pariza didn't ask any more questions. She just sat next to Abbu and started doodling.

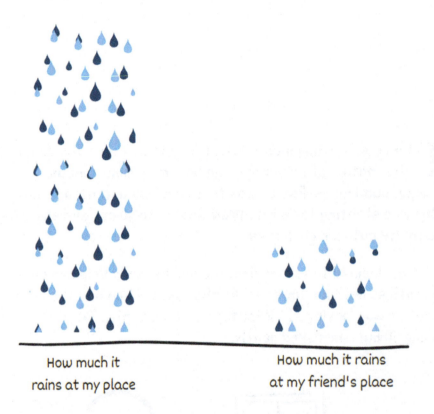

How much it rains at my place

How much it rains at my friend's place

After some time, Abbu noticed Pariza's sullen face and tried to cheer her up.

"What are you up to, Pariza?" he asked.

"Abbu, I called to check on Priya and it isn't raining at her place. They are going to the park. It just keeps raining here." Pariza was dejected.

Abbu chuckled at her innocence and asked her to show what she was drawing in her notebook. She shrugged her shoulders and handed over her notebook to Abbu. He looked at it and smiled.

"Abbu, is this a graph too?" Pariza asked.

"Well, it surely is. Looks like a bar graph of the amount of rain," he responded.

"Abbu, what if I want to do the same thing for all the cities in California or United States?" Pariza was getting excited.

"Well, if you want to do that, you'd need a bigger piece of paper." Abbu tried to explain. Showing data for many cities will need more space than a page of a notebook. "Or another idea is to create a map and use the amount of rain in each city as a data point."

Pariza was intrigued and eager to know more, "That sounds cool, Abbu! Can we do that?"

"Sure, we can start by making a simple map of United States. Then we will use a heatmap to show the amount of rainfall in different states," Abbu was happy to do anything to get Pariza cheer up especially if it's related to data.

Time Out!

A Heatmap is like a big coloring book page, but instead of coloring, we use colors to show how much of something there is in various parts of the picture. For example, we could use a heatmap to show how many people live in distinct parts of the world. A darker color could be used to show densely populated areas and a lighter color could be used to show a lesser populated area.

Heatmaps are useful because they help us see patterns and trends in data.

Pariza paused for a bit. She was clearly confused about something. "Abbu, I'm not sure we can use the amount of rain as our data set. It might be too hard to gather all that information for every state, don't you think?"

Abbu nodded in agreement. "You're right, Pariza. We need something simpler to work with." Pariza furrowed her brow, thinking hard. Suddenly, an idea struck her. "What if we use the number of letters in each state's name?" Dad smiled at her.

"That's a great idea, Pariza! That way we could create a color-coded map showing which states have the longest names. Let's get to work on it."

Abbu promptly fetched a printout of the map of United States.

They started by writing down the number of letters in each state on the map itself.

"Abbu, I just love Utah, Iowa, and Ohio. I wish all the states' names were just 4 letters long." Pariza giggled happily.

"Well, if all of those were only 4 letter long, you wouldn't get to color code them." Abbu chuckled with her.

"Oh, right! What do we do next? How to color code them?" Pariza was eager.

"This is going to be very interesting, Pariza. Pay close attention to this," said Abbu as he began creating a table.

"We can divide the states into three categories: states with names containing 4-6 letters, 7-9 letters, 10 or more letters."

"So, Oregon, Nevada and Idaho are going to be in one team?" asked Pariza curiously.

"Yes, next we will assign one color to each team."

Heatmap on a Rainy Day | 99

4-6 letters	Green
7-9 letters	Yellow
10 or more letters	Red

"Abbu, I can't wait to color and see what comes out of this."

After coloring the rest of the states based on the table Abbu had created, Pariza was finally done. She looked at the finished map and smiled at it.

"Abbu, this looks very colorful and since I know the meaning of these colors it is insightful as well," Pariza said with a sense of achievement.

"Yes Parizu, you could also add a key on the side so that anyone reading the graph can understand what these colors mean. This key is called a legend." Abbu encouraged her.

Pariza goes on to add a legend for the heatmap.

Heatmap on a Rainy Day | 101

Your turn to Play

Pariza is extremely excited about the new heatmap she learned in this chapter and requests Abbu to give her one more exercise.

"Pariza, I have an idea. Why don't you repeat what we did in this chapter but instead of counting the number of letters in state names, you can count the number of vowels in each state." Abbu suggested.

"I like it Abbu and then I can compare the final map with what we created earlier." Pariza remarked and got down to work.

"Excellent, but you would need to change the color code because the number of vowels would be less than total number of letters we used."

Can you help Pariza with this exercise? Count the number of vowels in each state's name and add it to the map below.

Create a color code with number of vowels to create the heatmap.

	Green
	Yellow
	Red

Color it as per the code you created above.

Take a close look at the map you colored and think about what it's telling you. Write down your thoughts.

----

12 MAPS & CHERRY BLOSSOMS

Pariza was elated when the sun finally shone after days of non-stop rain. The weekend had just begun, and she was showing off her martial arts moves to Abbu in the backyard.

"Abbu, Sensei taught us how to kick and quickly move back before someone grabs us," Pariza demonstrated.

"That's great, Pariza. It's always good to learn self-defense," Abbu responded, impressed by Pariza's swift movements.

He tried copying her moves, Pariza's younger brother joined in, and the three of them started a playful scuffle on the mat, laughing and having a wonderful time.

As they lay on the mat, Pariza pointed at the cherry blossoms in the tree and remarked, "Abbu, aren't they beautiful?"

"They certainly are, Pariza. I've always loved nature - the colors, the patterns, everything."

"Abbu, I miss Seattle. Remember when we used to go to that place full of cherry blossom trees?"

"Yes, the University of Washington. We had so much fun there. I'm sure there are a few other places famous for cherry blossoms in the US," Abbu replied.

Pariza remembering Cherry Blossoms Festival in Seattle

Abbu began searching for other popular locations to view cherry blossoms in the US and asked Pariza to fetch the map of the country. Together, they marked the locations on the map with a pencil. Pariza's younger brother couldn't comprehend much, and he started making funny faces and started putting cherry blossoms on the map.

"Abbu, look, he's ruining everything," Pariza grumbled, annoyed with her younger brother.

"Parizu, this is a wonderful idea. Instead of marking the places with pencil, we could instead mark it by putting a cherry blossom flower on the map," Abbu suggested.

"Really?" asked Pariza, intrigued.

"Yes, it's called physical data visualization. I saw something similar when we visited Salman uncle's place on Eid, and they had a map with pushpins placed on all the places they had traveled to," Abbu explained.

The trio continued to place the flowers on all the locations famous for cherry blossoms, creating a stunning visual representation of the popular destinations.

Best places to see Cherry Blossoms in USA

@drawing data with kids

Your turn to Play

Hope you enjoyed the cherry blossom map that Pariza created with Abbu. In the story above, Abbu also mentioned a map they saw at Salman uncle's place which had a pushpin for every place they had visited.

Take a printout of this map (or find a map of your country) and put a pin on all the places you have visited or would like to visit.

Take a close look at the graph you made and think about what it's telling you. Write down your thoughts and share with your family and friends.

EPILOGUE

Pariza woke up early one morning, her mind racing with excitement. She had learned lots of data visualization techniques in recent months and was eager to explore new inspirations on her upcoming journey to India.

As she looked over at her sleeping father, she couldn't help but notice the rhythm of his snores. It reminded her of the Snore Graph she created and how everyone laughed looking at it.

Glancing over at her mother, the way her hair fell in waves made her think of different line graph styles.

And as she looked at her younger brother sleeping peacefully beside her father, she remembered the different board games they analyzed and how he came out a winner in some of those.

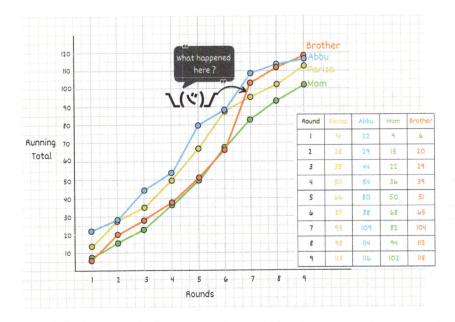

Pariza felt a sense of anticipation as she packed her bags and prepared for her trip. She couldn't wait to explore the vibrant colors, intricate patterns, and rich cultural history of India, and to see how she could incorporate these elements into her learning.

With a smile on her face, Pariza stepped out into the world, eager to continue her journey of learning, discovery, and creativity.

ACKNOWLEDGEMENT

I am grateful to my wife for her constant support, encouragement, and willingness to engage in countless discussions about data visualization. I want to thank my Parents for investing in me and getting me educated with limited resources they had. And I want to thank my kids for being my partner in the creation of this book and for their boundless curiosity and enthusiasm.

I am also deeply grateful to the Data Visualization Society for providing a platform for me to share my initial experiments in data visualization with my daughter. The feedback and encouragement from the community helped shape and refine the ideas presented in this book.

I would also like to thank my editor, Deepali Joshi Adhikary who provided invaluable guidance and support throughout the writing process.

Finally, I would like to acknowledge the work of the Late Dr Stanley Schmidt, whose writing of the 'Life of Fred' series inspired me to explore new ways of teaching complex topics in a fun and engaging way.

WHAT'S NEXT?

Thank You for reading 'Drawing Data with Kids.' I hope you found it informative, engaging, and fun! Moreover, I hope it helped you spend more offline time with your kids and teach them something new. I would love to hear your feedback on the book and any suggestions you may have for future editions.

Please scan the QR code below to take a brief survey and let me know your thoughts. As a token of appreciation, I will randomly select three survey participants to receive free enrollment to my upcoming workshops on Drawing Data with Kids.

Thank You again for your support and I look forward to hearing from you.

Made in the USA
Monee, IL
03 September 2023

42066996R00070